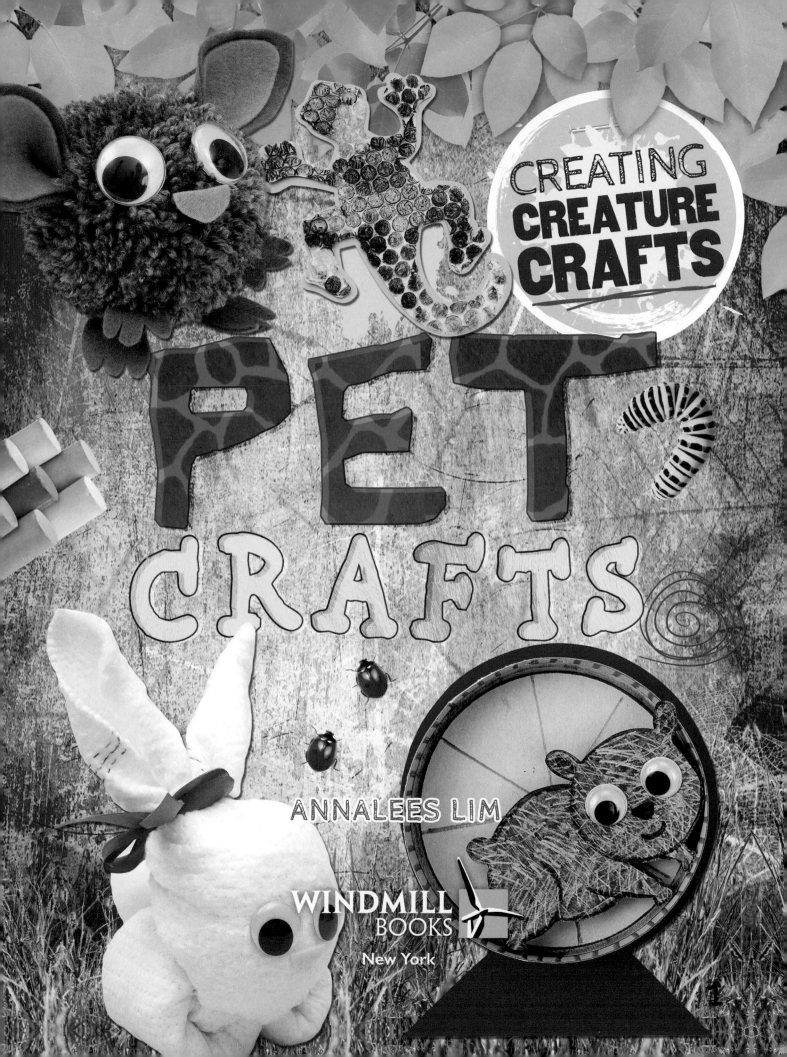

CREATING CREATURE CRAFTS

PET CRAFTS

ANNALEES LIM

WINDMILL
BOOKS
New York

CONTENTS

Welcome to the wonderful world of pets!

Do you have a pet? or is there perhaps a pet that you would really like to own? This book not only shows you how to make your very own crafty pets, it also tells you lots of fun facts about them along the way!

Follow the easy step-by-step instructions to start creating your own pet collection. When you have finished making an animal, you can also think about how it is kept and looked after.

A lot of the projects use paint and glue. Always cover surfaces with a piece of plastic or layers of old newspaper. Whenever you can, leave the project to dry before moving on to the next step. This keeps things from getting stuck to each other and paint from smudging.

A note about measurements

Measurements are given in U.S. form with metric in parentheses. The metric conversion is rounded to make it easier to measure.

So, do you have your craft tools ready to go? Then get set to make your crafty creatures and discover what makes each of them so special!

HAMSTER IN A WHEEL

Hamsters usually sleep in the day and play at night. But this hamster will be ready to spin in its wheel all day long!

1

Color the sheet of white paper in a layer of orange crayon. Then cover that layer completely with brown crayon.

2

Scratch off some of the brown crayon using the wooden toothpick. Make the scratches look like fur.

3

Use a black marker to draw a hamster shape, making sure you include small ears and legs. Cut out your hamster. Stick on the googly eyes with a glue stick.

4

Cut out a circle of red paper that is bigger than the round container. Stick the circle to the middle of the white card stock. Cut out a red paper triangle to form the base of the wheel.

5

Use the gray felt-tipped pen to draw spokes onto the wheel. Fix it to the middle of the red circle with the paper fastener. Glue the hamster to the wheel.

HAMSTER FACT
Did you know that hamsters can use pouches in their cheeks to store food?

POM-POM CHINCHILLA

Chinchillas live high up in the mountains. They have very soft, thick fur. Make your craft chinchilla just as fluffy by using soft yarn.

You will need:
Gray yarn
Card stock, 8½ by 11 inches (21.5 x 28cm)
Compass
Pencil
Scissors
Ruler
Dark and light gray felt
Fabric glue
Googly eyes

1

Fold the card stock in half. Draw a 2-inch-wide (5cm) circle, then a 6-inch-wide (15cm) circle around it. Cut around the edge of the large circle to make 2 circles. Fold the circles in half and cut the inside circle out of each of them.

2

Make a paper bobbin out of scrap card stock. Wrap some gray yarn around it, making sure it does not get bigger than the holes in the circles.

3

Place one circle on top of the other and start wrapping the yarn around them. Make sure there are no gaps in the yarn and that you wind 3 layers in total.

4

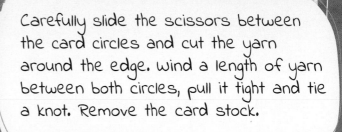

Carefully slide the scissors between the card circles and cut the yarn around the edge. Wind a length of yarn between both circles, pull it tight and tie a knot. Remove the card stock.

5

Cut out ears, a nose, front and back paws, and a tail from the felt. Stick them to the pom-pom with the fabric glue. Glue on the googly eyes.

CHINCHILLA FACT

A chinchilla's teeth never stop growing! They need to gnaw on wood to keep their teeth short.

POSH POODLE

Poodles are not just pretty to look at. They are one of the most intelligent dog breeds, too. Make your very own smart poodle to impress your friends!

You will need:
Card stock, 8½ by 11 inches (21.5 x 28cm)
Black marker
Cotton balls
Paint
Pot of water
Fabric glue
Glitter glue
Plastic bowl
Paintbrush
Scissors

1

Mix equal amounts of the paint and water in a bowl.

2

Soak 8 cotton balls in the paint mixture. Take them out and leave them to dry.

3

Use the black marker to draw the shape of a poodle on the card stock. Draw the face, two legs and the tail, leaving space for the body and head.

4

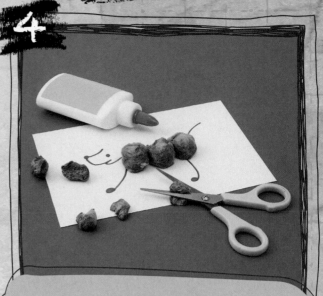

Stick the cotton balls onto the card stock using the fabric glue. They will form the ears, body, tail end and cuffs. You can make some smaller balls by cutting them up.

5

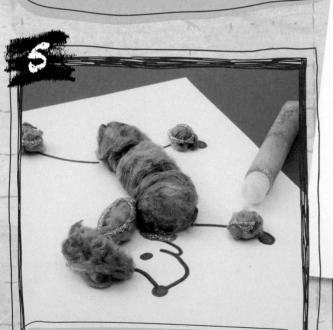

Decorate your poodle with glitter glue. Don't forget to add a collar, too.

POODLE FACT
Ancient Greeks used to keep pet poodles thousands of years ago!

GOOGLY-EYED GOLDFiSH

You will need:
Transparent plastic tub
3 small balloons
Orange tissue paper
Googly eyes
Modeling clay
Green tissue paper
Small stones
White glue, glue stick
Bowl of water
Paintbrush
Toothpicks
Scissors
Ruler

Goldfish are happiest when they are in a group. Make hese goldfish to go in your ank so that they can keep each other company.

1

Mix equal amounts of water and glue in a bowl. Blow up 3 balloons so they are no bigger than 2¾ inches (7cm) long.

2

Tear the orange tissue paper into small strips and dip each one into the glue-water mix. Stick them on the balloons until you have 3 layers of tissue paper. Leave to dry in a warm place.

3

When the tissue paper has dried, pop the balloons inside. Add some more tissue paper to each balloon to make fins and tails. Stick a pair of googly eyes to each fish.

4

Cut wavy shapes out of the green paper. Stick them around the inside of the plastic tub using a glue stick.

5

Press 3 chunks of modeling clay onto the bottom of the tub. Pierce the goldfish with toothpicks and stand them up in the modeling clay. Add small stones to the tub.

GOLDFISH FACT

Goldfish have great memories. This means it's possible to train a goldfish to do little tricks!

BUBBLE WRAP LIZARD

You will need:
Bubble Wrap
Glass paints
Scissors
Paper, 8½ by 11 inches
  (21.5 x 28cm)
Pencil
Paintbrush
Thick, colored
  card stock
Glue stick

A lizard's skin is not slimy, as you might think. It's very dry, and it is often bright and colorful. Use your favorite colors to decorate your lizard's skin.

1

Using a pencil, draw a lizard shape onto the paper to make a template. Cut it out with scissors.

2

Paint a pattern onto the Bubble Wrap using lots of different colors of glass paint. Leave to dry completely before moving on to the next step.

12

3

Stick the template to the Bubble wrap and carefully cut around the lizard shape.

4

Cut a lizard shape that is a bit bigger than your template out of the thick, colored card stock.

5

Stick the Bubble wrap lizard onto the colored card stock using a glue stick.

LIZARD FACT
If lizards lose their tail when they are being hunted, they can grow a new one!

FLUFFY BUNNY

Rabbits are born with their eyes closed and without fur. This fluffy bunny has its eyes wide open, lots of fur and is only slightly smaller than a real-life bunny!

1 Fold one of the white dustcloths in half. Fold the left edge towards the middle.

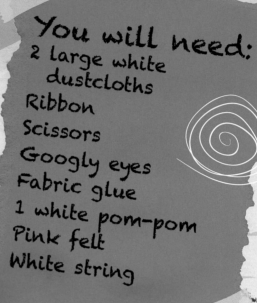

2 Fold the right edge over to the left side of the dustcloth.

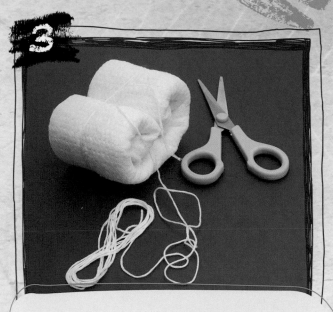

3

Roll the ends of the folded dustcloth towards each other. Tightly wrap a length of white string around it and secure with a strong knot. This will form your bunny's body.

4

Tie off two corners of the other dustcloth, using white string. These will form your bunny's ears. Roll the rest of the dustcloth together in a tight ball. Tie the ears together using ribbon.

5

Use fabric glue to stick your bunny's head to its body. Stick the pom-pom on to form the tail. Glue on the googly eyes and a nose cut out of pink felt.

BUNNY FACT

Rabbits can jump higher and further than a lot of humans can!

BEADY SNAKE

Some snakes can grow up to 30 feet (9m) long! You can make your snake as long as you like. Be sure to choose colorful fabric, too.

You will need:
Fabric, 12 by 2⅜ inch (30 x 6cm)
Lots of small beads (no wider than 3/4 inch or 2cm)
Fabric glue
Embroidery thread
Red felt
Scissors
2 small black beads
Measuring tape

1

Make a tube from the fabric and stick in place with the fabric glue. Also glue one end closed and leave to dry completely before moving on to the next step.

2

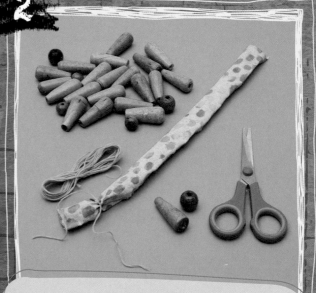

Put a few beads inside the fabric tube and tie a length of thread around the tube to hold them in place.

3

Repeat this for the rest of the tube until you have 1⅛ inch (3cm) of fabric left. Trim the end of the tube.

4

Wrap scrap fabric around a bead to form your snake's head. Tie the fabric together using embroidery thread. Glue the head to the body of your snake.

5

Cut out a tongue from the red felt and stick it to the head, using the fabric glue. Stick the black beads onto the side of the head to form your snake's eyes.

SNAKE FACT

Did you know that snakes can't chew? This means that they have to swallow their food whole!

FEATHERY PARAKEET

Parakeets have about 2,000–3,000 feathers! You can use just a handful to make your own colorful pet bird.

You will need:
Small polystyrene egg
Colored feathers
Yellow card stock
Craft glue
2 green pipe cleaners
Light blue acrylic paint
Paintbrush
Scissors
Googly eyes

1

Cut and bend each of the pipe cleaners to form a leg and claws. Stick them into the bottom of the polystyrene egg, so that it stands up.

2

Paint the egg in a layer of blue paint and leave it to dry.

3

Glue feathers to each side of the egg to make wings.

4

Cut out two yellow triangles, one slightly bigger than the other. Fold each triangle in half and then stick them onto the egg to form the beak.

5

Glue some googly eyes above your parakeet's beak.

PARAKEET FACT
Did you know that parakeets can learn how to say words and phrases?

PLAYFUL KITTEN

You will need:
Orange, white, pink and black foam
White glue
Scissors
Small ball of yarn
Stapler
Ruler

Kittens learn how to hunt by playing with their brothers and sisters. You can make your very own kitten that plays with a ball of yarn!

1

Cut an "H" shape out of orange foam. Make sure that the outline of the "H" is 2¾ (7cm) wide and 6 inches (15cm) tall.

2

Cut out an 8 by 2¾ inch (20 x 7cm) rectangle of orange foam for the body. Cut out a wavy shape that is 4 inches (10cm) tall to form the tail.

3

Shape the rectangle to form a tube and staple it together. Staple the "H" shape to the tube and staple the tail to the bottom of the "H."

4

Bend the 4 lengths of the "H" around the tube and staple them in place. Round off the ends of the lengths with scissors.

5

Make your kitten's face from foam and stick it together using glue. Glue the face to the top of the tube. You can also stick pink pads of foam to its paws. Place a ball of yarn between its paws.

CAT FACT

Did you know that cats sleep a lot more than we do? They nap for about 18 hours a day!

PUG POTS

In ancient China, pugs used to sit on the laps of emperors. You can make pug pots to sit on your desk and hold your pens!

1

Cut 2 toilet paper rolls so that they are different heights - one should be a bit shorter than the other.

2

Cover both cut rolls in cream paper. Cover the full-length roll in brown paper.

3

Make lots of small cuts into one end of each roll. Splay the ends out and stick the tubes onto the colored card stock.

4

Cut out two cream "u" shapes and one brown "u" shape. Cut out 4 small, cream-colored paws and 2 brown ones. Stick the shapes and paws to a pot of the same color.

5

Make a pug face for each of your pots by cutting out shapes from the colored paper. use your felt-tipped pen to add details. Stick each face onto a pot of the same color.

PUG FACT
Pugs have short noses. This means that they catch colds very easily.

GLOSSARY

bobbin   an object that has thread or yarn wound around it

emperor   a man who rules over a group of countries

intelligent   when a human or an animal is able to understand and learn things very well

template   a shape that is used as a guide to cut out something

INDEX

Published in 2016 by Windmill Books,
an Imprint of Rosen Publishing
29 East 21st Street, New York, NY 10010

Copyright © 2016 Wayland/Windmill

All rights reserved. No part of this book may be reproduced in any form without permission in writing from the publisher, except by a reviewer.

Series editor: Julia Adams
Craft photography: Simon Pask, N1 Studios
Additional images: Shutterstock

Cataloging-in-Publication Data
Lim, Annalees.
Pet crafts / by Annalees Lim.
p. cm. — (Creating creature crafts)
Includes index.
ISBN 978-1-5081-9109-4 (pbk.)
ISBN 978-1-5081-9110-0 (6-pack)
ISBN 978-1-5081-9111-7 (library binding)
1. Handicraft – Juvenile literature. 2. Pets – Juvenile literature. I. Lim, Annalees. II. Title.
TT160.L56 2016
745.592—d23

Manufactured in the United States of America
CPSIA Compliance Information Batch #BW16PK. For further information contact Rosen Publishing, New York, New York at 1-800-237-9932.